PLAY ALONG WITH THE CANADIAN BRASS

THE CANADIAN
BRASS

17 EASY PIECES

Trumpets: Jens Lindemann, Ron Romm
Horn: Chris Cooper
Trombone: Gene Watts
Tuba: Chuck Daellenbach

Contents

The five solo books may be played as an exsemble. Each solo book's CD includes a version of each piece with the featured part omitted.

Recorded March 8, 1999, Toronto; Edward Marshall, engineer

HAL•LEONARD® CORPORATION

7777 W. BLUEMOUND RD. P.O. BOX 13819 MILWAUKEE, WI 53213

Visit Hal Leonard Online at
www.halleonard.com
Visit Canadian Brass online at
www.canbrass.com

JUST A CLOSER WALK

Traditional American
Arranged by Don Gillis
Adapted by Walter Barnes

TWO CHORALES
1. O Sacred Head

Johann Sebastian Bach
(1685-1750)
Arranged by Charles Sayre

Legato tongue throughout unless otherwise slurred.

2. Break Forth, O Beauteous Heavenly Light

SAKURA
(Cherry Blossoms)

Traditional Japanese Folksong
Arranged by Walters Barnes

HOSANNA

Giovanni Pierluigi da Palestrina
(1525-1594)
Arranged by Walter Barnes

NON NOBIS DOMINE

William Byrd
(1543-1623)
Arranged by Walter Barnes

This is a CANON at the 5th and 8ve.
If you wish to repeat, (go around again,) then stop at the asterisk mark (*) and go immediately to your first note, ignoring the preceding rest (s). Conclude at the double bar.

MY COUNTRY 'TIS OF THEE/GOD SAVE THE QUEEN

from *Thesaurus Musicus*, 1744
Arranged by Walter Barnes

SAINT ANTHONY

Franz Joseph Haydn
(1732-1809)
Arranged by Walter Barnes

28 Saint Anthony *continued*

STEAL AWAY

African-American Spiritual
Arranged by Walter Barnes

CANON

Thomas Tallis
(c1505-1585)
arranged by Charles Sayre

*Legato Tongue all note,
unless otherwise indicated

ODE TO JOY
(from Symphony No. 9)

Ludwig van Beethoven
(1770-1827)
Arranged by Walter Barnes

ETERNAL FATHER, STRONG TO SAVE
(Navy Hymn)

John B. Dykes, c1861
Arranged by Rick Walters

LARGO
(Ombra mai fù from the opera *Xerxes*)

George Frideric Handel
(1685-1759)
Arranged by Walter Barnes

MUSIC FROM THE ROYAL FIREWORKS

George Frideric Handel
(1685-1759)
Arranged by Walter Barnes

GREENSLEEVES

16th Century English Song
Arranged by Terry Vosbein

TRUMPET VOLUNTARY

Jeremiah Clarke
(1673-1707)
Arranged by Walter Barnes

Allargando

IN THE HALL OF THE MOUNTAIN KING

Edvard Grieg
(1843-1907)
Arranged by Charles Sayre

*Sempre Staccato